LIGHTHOUSES OF WISCONSIN

Help Us Keep This Guide Up to Date

Every effort has been made by the authors and editors to make this guide as accurate and useful as possible. However, many things can change after a guide is published—phone numbers change, facilities come under new management, etc.

We would love to hear from you concerning your experiences with this guide and how you feel it could be improved and be kept up to date. While we may not be able to respond to all comments and suggestions, we'll take them to heart, and we'll also make certain to share them with the authors. Please send your comments and suggestions to the following address:

The Globe Pequot Press
Reader Response/Editorial Department
P. O. Box 480
Guilford, CT 06437

Or you may e-mail us at:

editorial@GlobePequot.com

Thanks for your input, and happy travels!

LIGHTHOUSES OF WISCONSIN

A Guidebook and Keepsake

Bruce Roberts and Ray Jones

INSIDERS' GUIDE®

GUILFORD, CONNECTICUT
AN IMPRINT OF THE GLOBE PEQUOT PRESS

To buy books in quantity for corporate use or incentives, call **(800) 962–0973, ext. 4551,** or e-mail **premiums@GlobePequot.com.**

INSIDERS' GUIDE®

Text design by Schwartzman Design, Deep River, CT
Map design and terrain by Stephen C. Stringall, Cartography by M. A. Dubé
Maps © 2006 Morris Book Publishing, LLC.
All photographs are by Bruce Roberts unless otherwise credited.

Library of Congress Cataloging-in-Publication Data
Roberts, Bruce, 1930-
  Lighthouses of Wisconsin: a guidebook and keepsake / Bruce Roberts and Ray Jones.—1st ed.
    p. cm. – (Lighthouses series)
  ISBN 0-7627-3969-X
 1. Lighthouses–Wisconsin–Guidebooks. I. Jones, Ray, 1948- II. Title. III. Lighthouses series (Globe Pequot Press)

  VK1024.W6R63 2005
  386'.855'09775–dc22

                                                            2005013174

Manufactured in China
First Edition/First Printing

The information listed in this guide was confirmed at press time. The ownership of many lighthouses, however, is gradually being transferred from the Coast Guard to private concerns. Please confirm visitor information before traveling.

DEDICATION

To Rick Polad, a friend of lighthouses and a friend to me
—Bruce Roberts

To Barry Yarbro
—Ray Jones

ACKNOWLEDGMENTS

My thanks to the talented photographers who provided pictures:
Rick Polad and Sandra and Bob Shanklin, "The Lighthouse People."
My special gratitude to Dave Snyder, formerly with the National
Park Service, who provided transportation to the lighthouses of the
Apostle Islands. Thanks also to Ann Hoge and Fran Platske,
daughters of lighthouse keepers.
—Bruce Roberts

The Baileys Harbor rear-range lighthouse was once used as a Lutheran parsonage. Rick Polad

CONTENTS

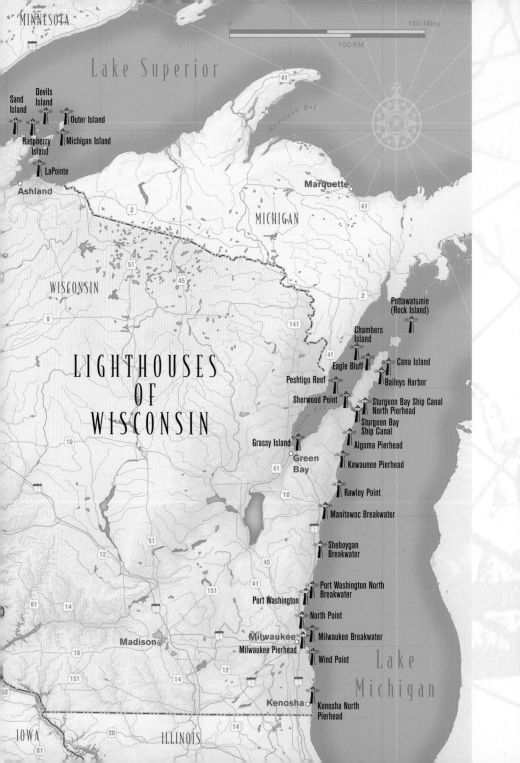

INTRODUCTION

T he Ojibwa and other ancient mariners who braved America's inland seas often turned their eyes to the sky for guidance. Sailors, no matter what seas they've sailed, have always used the night skies as a kind of celestial map. Even with all the finely calibrated compasses, radar, and other sophisticated electronic direction-finding equipment found on the bridges of ships nowadays, sea captains and lake sailors still occasionally take a reading on the stars. But while the sailor's friend, old reliable Polaris, can point the way north, it cannot warn of a dangerous shoal, help navigate a narrow, rock-strewn channel, or mark the passage to a safe harbor. For these purposes sailors have long looked to certain man-made "stars" along the shore.

Sailors were already braving the earth's open waters long before the dawn of civilization. When caught in the dark, they used the faint glow of firelight from coastal encampments or villages to help them find their way to shore. The earliest maritime peoples may have banked fires on the hillsides to call their sailors home from the sea. When towns and cities grew up, lamps were placed in towers or other high places to make their harbors easier to find at night.

The world's first true lighthouse was erected in about 280 B.C. at Alexandria, the old Greco-Egyptian trading center at the mouth of the Nile. It stood on an island called Pharos, near the entrance to Alexandria's bustling harbor. Towering some 450 feet above the Mediterranean Sea, it was the tallest lighthouse ever built and the one with the longest service record.

At night keepers lit bright fires at the top of the huge tower to guide Phoenicians, Greeks, Carthaginians, Romans, and other mariners from all over the known world to this fabled and prosperous city. Most came to load their ships with food grown in the Nile delta. The rich soil of the delta was so wondrously productive that its grains fed Roman legions and city dwellers all around the Mediterranean basin and made possible the Roman Empire. But the grain would never have reached market without the enormous lighthouse that guided sea captains and their freight ships into and out of Alexandria. The Pharos lighthouse served faithfully for more than a thousand years until a powerful earthquake toppled it near the end of the first millennium.

Lights at the Edge of an Inland Sea

Like the Mediterranean of ancient times, North America's inland seas are, today, a heavily traveled thoroughfare. Great Lakes freighters carry an endless variety of raw materials and finished products—iron ore to steel mills, metal parts to auto assembly plants, oil and chemicals to refineries, and grain from the prodigious farms of the Midwest to hungry people all over the world.

The Great Lakes have been a driving force in the American economy. Long lake freighters, together with their brave crews, have fueled the nation's economic engine, but the prosperity brought by commerce has come at a high price: thousands of ships sunk and many more thousands of sailors drowned or frozen to death in the lakes' dark and frigid waters. The cost in vessels and lives would have been much higher if not for the sparkling constellation of lighthouses that ring each of the Great Lakes.

For more than a century and a half, lake sailors have been guided by a linked chain of navigational lights extending more than 1,200 miles from the St. Lawrence River to Duluth. Many of the lights have shined out over the lake waters since America itself was young, and most are at least a century old. All have played an essential role in the economic development and history of the United States.

Some of the brightest and most interesting Great Lakes lighthouses mark the shores of Wisconsin. Those not familiar with America's inland seas might not think of these heart-of-America Midwestern states as rich in maritime commerce and tradition, but they would be wrong. Milwaukee has long ranked among our nation's most important ports, and there are many other smaller but nonetheless important ports along the Wisconsin lakeshores. Some are places with interesting Native American names, such as Kenosha, Sheboygan, Manitowoc, and Algoma, suggesting that they were once frequented by Indian canoes rather than block-long lake freighters. One thing all Midwestern ports, whether great or small, have in common is the fact that they would never have grown up and prospered without navigational lights.

The Great Lakes have always presented a special challenge for sailors. Because they are located near the center of one of the earth's largest landmasses, the weather patterns that sweep across the lakes are quite different from—and often more violent than—

those encountered on the open ocean. North America receives heavier snows than any other continent, so the lakes are the snowiest navigable bodies of water on the planet.

But potentially blinding snow squalls are only one of the lake sailor's many concerns. Storms driven by the sharp temperature differences over land and over water can strike swiftly and with extraordinary intensity. Skies may clear again in a matter of minutes, or the heavy weather may go on for days. Since freshwater is lighter than salt water, wind-driven waves that batter the sides of ships tend to mount higher. The lakes' narrow widths and even narrower channels leave ships little room to maneuver. And there are countless ship-killing shoals and low, almost invisible headlands waiting to devour any vessel and crew that stray too far off course.

The photogenic Cana Island Lighthouse is located in beautiful Door County, home to an impressive array of historic maritime towers.

Ships are still occasionally lost on the lakes today. Indeed, the lakes are so unpredictable and, at times, so dangerous that regular commercial shipping would be impossible without an extensive, well-planned system of navigational aids. Fortunately, just such a network exists to make the work of lake sailors easier and safer. With buoys, channel lights, and an endless variety of other maritime signposts, the U.S. and Canadian Coast Guards have turned the lakes into a well-marked superhighway. One might almost think that lake navigators should

stow their charts and compasses and buy road maps, but of course, piloting a 40,000-ton ore freighter is a bit more complicated and touchy than driving the family Winnebago.

Lighthouses were once indispensable to the Great Lakes navigational network, but their importance has diminished. Twenty-first-century radar, the satellite-assisted Global Positioning System (GPS), and a bewildering array of high-tech, shipboard devices have made pinpoint navigation not only possible, but commonplace. Rendered all but obsolete, lighthouse beacons have been relegated to a secondary navigational role. Even so, mariners still rely on them. Despite changing times and technologies, for mariners one thing has remained constant throughout the ages: They are on their own. That is why most of the time—and always in a storm—sailors trust their eyes and their instincts more than any digital readout. So

on a dark night or in a gale, when captains or pilots are seen with binoculars in hand, they are most likely scanning the horizon in search of a lighthouse beacon.

Automation: The End of an Era

Undertaken for efficiency's sake, the process of automation began during the early twentieth century and accelerated dramatically after 1950. One by one, America's fine old lighthouse keeper's residences were boarded up or torn down, and operation of the lights was turned over to machinery. By the end of the 1960s, most of Wisconsin's lighthouses had been automated. Automated in 1926, the Eagle Bluff Light became one of the first on the Great Lakes to operate without a full-time keeper, while the keepers at Sherwood Point Light held out until 1983.

Nowadays historic navigational lights such as those shining from North Point in Milwaukee, Cana Island in Door County, and Michigan Island in the Apostles receive their instructions by radio or from computer programs. Coast Guard operators and maintenance personnel need to visit these stations only occasionally. But for more than a century, these lights were tended manually by keepers who lived and worked on-site. Although their families often lived with them, theirs was a very lonely existence.

It might logically be assumed that the keepers, because of their choice of profession, were hermits—lovers of craggy, storm-beaten rocks unpopulated except for birds, lichens, and themselves. Like most simplistic notions, however, this one is false. Generally speaking, people accepted work as lighthouse keepers not because they were antisocial but because it was a job. It offered them steady employment, certain if moderate pay, and a place to live.

Often keepers and their families suffered greatly from loneliness, especially at remote stations such as those in the Apostle Islands. Today, however, keepers no longer need to endure such isolation—nor do they enjoy the splendors of it. Indeed, for all practical purposes, the profession of lighthouse keeper is extinct in America. But it is far from forgotten. Living at the very edge of the sea and maintaining their lifesaving sentinels, the keepers and their lighthouses appeal to our romantic instincts.

A blaze of fall color brightens the Cana Island tower. It is easy to see why lighthouses are a favorite subject of photographers. Rick Polad

How to Use This Guide

Dozens of lighthouses once marked the rugged lakeshores of the Upper Midwest. Not all are still standing, and more than a few have been taken out of service and allowed to go dark. But a surprising number of the region's historic lighthouses have survived, in some

cases for more than a century, the ravages of wind and weather. Many of the old lights are still burning, offering guidance to any mariner, whether aboard a 900-foot-long lake freighter or a 12-foot fishing boat. Even today, none but the most foolish sailor would ignore their warnings.

Through words and pictures, this book gives the reader a look at these unique structures as well as a glimpse at their fascinating histories—each, as you'll see, has its own rich story to tell. Here you can read the stories and learn the facts. Then, if you wish, you can stake your claim to a share of the region's rich maritime heritage by going out to visit a Great Lakes lighthouse.

This book takes you to every Wisconsin lighthouse that can be reached and to some that are inaccessible. As you'll see, the book is divided into three sections: Pointing the Way to Milwaukee: From Kenosha to Algoma, Doorway to Green Bay: From Sturgeon Bay to Green Bay, and Lights of the Apostles: From Michigan Island to Sand Island. Within the sections lighthouses are presented in geographic order, just as they might appear on the map. This arrangement should make it easier for you to plan your own Wisconsin lighthouse outings—so should the directions, telephone contacts, and other travel information included at the end of each listing.

Under normal circumstances you should be able to visit the most attractive lighthouses in one or another of the sections mentioned above in a single long weekend excursion from Milwaukee or Green Bay. To help you select the lighthouses you want to visit, individual listings include advice in the form of simple symbols: ▣ for lighthouses that are especially historic—most of them are; ⚓ for lighthouses that are accessible—more than a few are not; ▨ for visitor-friendly lighthouses that are frequently open to the public and feature museums or similar attractions; and ▣ for lighthouses that make great pictures—most of them are quite photogenic. For added convenience, each listing also includes an easy-to-read summary of key information on the lighthouse: location, date the light was established, current status, height of the tower, type of optic, range, characteristic, elevation of the beacon, and, for all active lighthouses, the precise latitude and longitude of the station.

We hope you enjoy your Wisconsin lighthouse adventure.

CHAPTER ONE
POINTING THE WAY TO MILWAUKEE:
FROM KENOSHA TO ALGOMA

L ighthouse history in the Upper Midwest dates back roughly 170 years to 1836 and the construction of the Root River Lighthouse south of Milwaukee. Built with a stingy congressional appropriation of $5,000, this early navigational station consisted of a stubby 34-foot tower and a modest keeper's residence. The outmoded oil lamp–and–reflector optic inside the birdcage-like lantern atop the tower produced a relatively dim light, but even so, the new beacon helped turn a remote trading post into the bustling port of Racine.

Within two years of the establishment of the Root River Light, Milwaukee had a lighthouse of its own, and during the years and decades that followed, ports, harbors, and dangerous navigational obstacles all along the shores of Wisconsin were marked with lighthouses. In time, the state fairly sparkled at night. No one can say for sure how many ships and lives these lights saved over the years, but if the number were known, it would be impressive.

It is important to remember, however, that the lighthouses themselves could not have done the all-important job of marking the lakeshores alone. A lighthouse, after all, is only a tall building equipped with a lighting apparatus. It took a keeper, and oftentimes the keeper's family as well, to properly tend a navigational beacon.

Until shortly before World War II, all U.S. keepers were members of the Lighthouse Service, a federal government agency dating to the earliest years of the republic. A far-flung affair, the service built and maintained light stations in the east from Maine to Florida; in the west from San Diego to Anchorage, Alaska; and along the Great Lakes from the Lake Ontario entrance to the St. Lawrence River all the way to the far end of Lake Superior.

Of course, not all members of the service were lighthouse keepers. Some were bureaucrats and accountants in Washington, D.C., others were warehousemen and longshoremen who stockpiled supplies at Lighthouse Service depots, while still others were sailors aboard the vessels that delivered the food, coal, oil, and other necessities that fed keepers and their families and kept the lights burning. As the following section reveals, some honorary members of the Lighthouse Service were not even people.

A Sea Dog Returns to the Water

Traditionally, the small freighters and work ships known as light-house tenders were given the names of flowers, such as *Marigold, Orchid,* or *Azalea.* During the early decades of the twentieth century, the tender *Hyacinth,* operating out of Milwaukee and Chicago, served many of the lake lighthouses, especially those on Lake Michigan. Lighthouse keepers were always happy to see the *Hyacinth* steaming toward them with her cargo of fresh food and sorely needed supplies. No doubt the lonely keepers were also glad to have visitors and enjoyed sharing news, a scrap or two of gossip, and a hot mug of coffee with the captain and crew of the *Hyacinth.*

Rawley Point's three separate gallery rings give it an ornate appearance, not unlike that of a wedding cake.

For more than a dozen years, Sport, a spotted mongrel, sailed with the *Hyacinth,* making friends everywhere he went. When he died of old age, the following elegy appeared in the September 1926 *Lighthouse Bulletin* (a publication once distributed monthly by the Lighthouse Service):

To the Superintendent of Lighthouses, Milwaukee, Wisconsin

Sport was just a dog, but he was always a good dog and a good shipmate, a friend to everybody and everybody's friend. . . .
Sport came on board this vessel back in 1914 when engineer Albert Collins pulled him out of the Milwaukee River during a thunderstorm. He was in a pitiful condition and practically skin and bones. He was rescued and fed, and apparently, from that moment on, never had a notion to leave the ship.
Many things have happened to Sport and he has figured in many happenings aboard the ship in the 12 years he spent on board, which is longer than any officer or member of the crew has been here. It will not do to go into all the details of his life for they are many. It is enough to say that when he was in his prime there was no place on the ship that he did not visit and nothing going on that he did not have a hand or paw in. He swam and played baseball with the boys.

No boat could go ashore without Sport, and on many occasions he has carried a heaving line to shore in the breakers when landing on the beach at some light station with our crew.

He was lost in Chicago on one occasion and could not be found. We were a sad lot when we left Chicago without him and a happy lot when . . . the captain of the passenger steamer *Indiana* called me on the telephone to tell me he had Sport on board and to come over and get him. It was learned afterwards that someone had tied him up in a barn in Chicago, and it so happened that a man who had been a fireman on board [the *Hyacinth*] was driving an ice wagon and found Sport and brought him back to our Chicago pier keeper who in turn gave him to Captain Redner on the *Indiana* to deliver to us in Milwaukee. All of which goes to show that he had friends everywhere.

Sport died of old age on July 19, 1926. He was sewed in canvas and buried at sea the following afternoon. All hands were mustered on the spar deck where, with a few words for Sport to the effect that he had been taken from the waters and was now being returned to them, he was slid off the gangplank by a bunch of solemn-looking boys. He was given a salute and thus ended Sport, the best dog I have ever known.

This square tower has guarded Kewaunee harbor's south pier for more than seventy years.

Sport was not the only one pulled out of a cold river by a *Hyacinth* seaman. About the time the old sea dog took his last journey, his human friends on the *Hyacinth* were making daring rescues. In 1926 in Green Bay, Wisconsin, fireman Louis Ettenhoffer rescued a six-year-old boy who had fallen out of a small boat. It was early evening and Ettenhoffer was going ashore

to enjoy what for him was a rare treat—a home-cooked meal at his
sister's house. No sooner had his feet hit the dock than he noticed
the struggling child. Ettenhoffer was himself a very poor swimmer,
but he jumped into the river immediately and grabbed the boy just
in time to keep him from sinking. Somehow he reached a piling
and held on to it with one hand and the boy with the other until
both he and the child could be rescued by other members of the
Hyacinth crew.

In his report on the incident, the *Hyacinth*'s master, Captain
H. W. Maynard, noted that "the boy had swallowed some water but
was not harmed." As for Ettenhoffer, said the captain, "He had done
about all the swimming he was capable of doing and had
consumed a great plenty of the Fox River's water. He, however,
changed his clothes and kept his dinner engagement."

Later in 1926, while tied up at a dock to service a lighthouse
at Sturgeon Bay, Wisconsin, the *Hyacinth* almost became the first
lighthouse tender to be hit by a car. Crewmen heard the roar of an
engine and looked up in astonishment from their chores to see an
automobile racing along the pier and bearing down on their ship.
Luckily, the speeding car missed the *Hyacinth;* but, unfortunately for
the driver, it ran right off the end of the dock into Sturgeon Bay.
Although the car sank immediately, crewmen could see its lights
still burning under the water. Working quickly, they managed to
snare the vehicle with a grappling hook and use the tender's hoist
to pull the car out of the bay. Unhappily, their efforts were not in
time to save the hapless driver. No one ever knew why he drove his
car off the dock.

Even without flying cars, working on a lighthouse tender could
be quite dangerous. Sailors occasionally drowned when swells
overturned the small boats they used for landing passengers and
supplies at remote lighthouses. Others were killed while trying to
rescue the crews of wrecked ships. Some died in falls or when
swept overboard by high waves.

Although dangerous, the work of lighthouse keepers and the
sailors who manned the lighthouse tenders that helped keep the
lights burning was essential to the safe navigation of the Great
Lakes. Without their efforts and the sacrifices they made, the
United States would not be the prosperous nation it is today, for
the commerce carried out on the lakes was a vital part of the
engine that drove the American economy during the nineteenth and
twentieth centuries.

KENOSHA NORTH PIERHEAD LIGHT

Built in 1906, the Kenosha North Pierhead Light is still an official Coast Guard beacon. It serves as part of a range-light system to help mariners stay within the narrow approach channel. The station's red, cast-iron tower stands at the end of a harbor pier.

Just down the beach from the pierhead light, Kenosha's Simmons Island Park is home to "Old" Southport Lighthouse, so designated because it was out of service for nearly a century. Built in 1866, just after the Civil War, the 55-foot brick tower marked Kenosha Harbor for more than forty years. It was decommissioned in 1906 after construction of the Kenosha North Pierhead Light. The Kenosha County Historical Society has recently restored the old tower and adjacent dwelling. The light has been restored and now functions as a private aid to navigation.

TO SEE THE LIGHT: The pierhead lighthouse is located at the far end of the North Pier in Kenosha; the tower is accessible by foot. To visit the Old Southport Lighthouse, follow Fiftieth Street to Simmons Island Park, and then take Fourth Avenue and Simmons Island Road.

Location: Kenosha

Established: 1866

Tower height: 50 feet

Elevation of the focal plane: 50 feet

Optic: Modern

Status: Active

Characteristic: Red interrupted every 6 seconds

Range: 12 miles

Position: 42° 35' 20
87° 48' 31

Note: Took the place of the Southport Light

The red-towered Kenosha Pierhead Light and automated breakwater light (opposite right) guide vessels into the harbor, while the Old Southport tower (above) now graces a Kenosha city park.

Rick Polad

WIND POINT LIGHT

Immediately after the Civil War, a pier light was built to guide ships into Racine Harbor. The beacon was never totally satisfactory, however, since Wind Point blocked the light from the view of navigators piloting vessels approaching from the north. To correct this problem, Congress appropriated $100,000 for construction of a fine new lighthouse on the point.

Begun in 1877 and completed three years later, the Wind Point Light was fitted with a pair of lenses. Its third-order Fresnel lens displayed a flashing white light, while a smaller fifth-order lens marked the dangerous Racine Shoals with a red light. The station is now automated, and its unusual double-lens optic has been replaced by an airport-style beacon. The brick tower is 108 feet tall and attached by a passageway to its two-story dwelling.

TO SEE THE LIGHT: From Highway 32 south of Milwaukee, follow Three Mile Road and Lighthouse Drive to the station. The grounds are open to the public, but not the tower. The town of Wind Point uses the lighthouse for offices. From Racine's Lake Festival Park, visitors can see the 40-foot tower of the old Racine North Breakwater Light (1903) and the more recently constructed skeleton tower of the Racine South Breakwater Light. From Highway 32 turn toward the lake on Fourth Street.

Location: Racine

Established: 1866

Tower height: 108 feet

Elevation of the focal plane: 111 feet

Optic: Airport-style beacon

Status: Active

Characteristic: Flashes every 20 seconds

Range: 28 miles

Position: 42° 56' 52
87° 45' 30

Note: Among the most powerful beacons on the Great Lakes

Although lighthouses are utilitarian structures, some are endowed with lovely architectural details.

NORTH POINT LIGHTHOUSE

Built several years before the Civil War, Milwaukee's first lighthouse served for more than thirty years before erosion undercut the structure. A second tower, erected alongside the first, was ready for service in 1888. Similar in design, these early towers were octagonal and made of cast iron or steel.

The 1888 tower was only 35 feet tall, and within two decades spreading tree limbs began to obscure its beacon. In 1912 lighthouse engineers came up with a novel way to solve this problem. Rather than build an entirely new tower, they constructed a broad octagonal base, about 40 feet high, and then placed the original tower on top of it. In this way the overall height was raised to 74 feet.

Having helped mark the entrance to the Milwaukee River for more than a century, the North Point Lighthouse was deactivated in 1994. Both the tower and the spacious keeper's dwelling, dating from 1855, remain standing.

TO SEE THE LIGHT: The lighthouse is located in Lake Park, just off Wahl Avenue in Milwaukee. Follow Lincoln Memorial Drive to McKinley Park, then North Terrace to North Wahl Avenue.

Location: Milwaukee

Established: 1855

Tower height: 74 feet

Elevation of the focal plane: 154 feet

Status: Deactivated in 1994

Note: Stacked towers

North Point hasn't changed much since a 1912 renovation doubled the height of the tower.
U.S. Coast Guard

Rick Polad

MILWAUKEE PIERHEAD LIGHT

Location: Milwaukee

Established: 1872

Tower height: 42 feet

Elevation of the focal
plane: 45 feet

Optic: Modern

Status: Active

Characteristic: Flashes
red every 4 seconds

Range: 12 miles

Position: 43° 02' 41
87° 52' 48

Note: Marks the
Milwaukee Harbor
entrance

Like so many other pierhead lighthouses on the Great Lakes, this one is painted red for better visibility. Located at the end of a lengthy pier, the 42-foot, garishly painted tower has marked the entrance to Milwaukee's harbor for a century. Built in 1906, it replaced an earlier structure, which had served the same purpose since 1872. The tower owes its durability to its sturdy cast-iron construction. The station's original fourth-order Fresnel lens was eventually exchanged for a small fifth-order lens. Nowadays, however, a modern optic produces the beacon.

TO SEE THE LIGHT: The tower can be reached via a long walk along the harbor pier accessed through Milwaukee's Festival Park. The station's old Fresnel lens is now on display at the Wisconsin Maritime Museum in Manitowoc; call (920) 684–0218.

Rick Polad

MILWAUKEE BREAKWATER LIGHT

Location: Milwaukee

Established: 1926

Tower height: 53 feet

Elevation of the focal
plane: 61 feet

Optic: Modern

Status: Active

Characteristic: Flashes
red every 10 seconds

Range: 14 miles

Position: 43° 01' 37
87° 52' 55

Note: Square tower on
top of blocky keeper's
dwelling

Bob and Sandra Shanklin, The
Lighthouse People

Often harbors are protected from high waves by a lengthy barrier of stone called a breakwater. Because they rise only a few feet at most above the surface, breakwaters are hard to see, especially at night, and may threaten vessels entering or exiting the harbor. Breakwater beacons, like this one in Milwaukee, are meant to make mariners aware of this hazard and help them safely navigate the harbor entrance. For obvious reasons, the light tower usually is placed near the end of the breakwater.

Built in 1926, the rather blocky Milwaukee Breakwater Light owes its unusual appearance to the era of art deco. The stout concrete building consists of a square tower placed on top of the station quarters. No keeper has lived here since 1966, when the Coast Guard automated this light.

TO SEE THE LIGHT: The squared-off Milwaukee Breakwater Light cannot be reached from land, but it can be seen from the harbor pier, which reaches out into Lake Michigan from Festival Park.

WHAT IS A LIGHTHOUSE?

The term *lighthouse* has been applied to a wide variety of buildings constructed for the purpose of guiding ships. Often it is used interchangeably with similar or derivative terms such as *light tower* or *light station.* However, our usual concept of a lighthouse is that of a residence with a light tower either attached or located a short distance away. Even so, many so-called lighthouses never really fit this description.

While ancient Alexandria's Pharos tower is said to have been the world's first lighthouse, no evidence exists that keepers ever used any part of this colossal stone building as a residence. Keepers might have lived there, but who can say? The Statue of Liberty's torch once helped guide New York City harbor traffic, but is the big bronze lady really a lighthouse? Some would say so. Others maintain that a real light "house" must, naturally enough, have a residence associated with it. Nearly all of Wisconsin's lighthouses had a residence at one time or another.

Early coastal beacons were mostly open fires set blazing on top of a tall building or at the summit of a hill. Usually, these rather primitive beacons were operated by port authorities, maritime guilds, or local merchants who hoped to promote commerce. The "keepers" they hired or, in places where slavery was common, forced to tend the fires might or might not live near the place where they worked. Later, as more and more beacons were established

Sherwood Point Light illustrates a light station in which the tower is attached to the keeper's dwelling—a true lighthouse.

on islands or in other remote locations, the residences of keepers and the towers where they tended their lights became more closely identified. By the seventeenth or eighteenth century, the notion of a lighthouse as a dwelling with a light tower had become more or less fixed.

In 1915 the government saw the need to carefully define some of the terms commonly used in its published manuals and regulations. The U.S. Bureau of Lighthouses defined *lighthouse* as a "light station where a resident keeper is employed." Bureau lighthouses usually included one or more residences, a light tower (either attached to or separate from the keeper's dwelling), a storage facility for oil and other supplies, and sometimes a separate building to house foghorn machinery. To help the keepers feed themselves and their families, the light station property often had a garden patch, a chicken coop, and even a barn for cows.

Today the U.S. Coast Guard refers to the major beacons on its official list simply as *lights,* and many of these are a far cry from what once might have been described as a lighthouse. For instance, many Midwestern navigational lights, including several in Wisconsin, consist of little more than a small light perched atop a massive concrete fog-signal building. Such lights are automated and function without the daily assistance of keepers. In fact, as with maritime lights on every coast throughout the United States, all of Wisconsin's navigational lights are now automated.

The Racine North Breakwater Light is a simple steel structure with no support facilities.
Rick Polad

PORT WASHINGTON LIGHTHOUSE

Location: Port
Washington

Established: 1860

Status: Deactivated
in 1903

Note: Now an attractive
museum

Built in 1860, only about a year before the outbreak of the
Civil War, the Port Washington light station marked a small
but busy harbor a few miles north of Milwaukee. The lighthouse stood on a bluff overlooking the town. Shining from atop
a small tower rising from the pitched roof of the two-story brick
station dwelling, the light guided vessels in and out of the
harbor and along the nearby lakeshore.

During the 1930s the government built a lengthy stone
breakwater to protect the harbor from the high waves generated
by Lake Michigan's prodigious storms. When the breakwater
was completed in 1935, a light tower was placed at its far end,
rendering the original station obsolete. Although the tower was
removed from its roof long ago, the old keeper's dwelling still
stands. Located not far from the Port Washington business
district, it serves as a museum and as home to the Port
Washington Historical Society, which has restored the building
to its original appearance. The station's rooftop tower has been
replaced. Oddly enough, money for the restoration was donated
by the government of Luxembourg.

Before the Port
Washington Historical
Society restored the lighthouse (shown below in
2001), it had fallen into
disrepair and even lost its
tower.

TO SEE THE LIGHT: The Old Port Washington Lighthouse Museum
is located at Johnson
and Power Streets in
downtown Port
Washington; visit
www.lighthouse
friends.com.

Linda Nenn

PORT WASHINGTON NORTH BREAKWATER LIGHT

📷
Location: Port
Washington

Established: 1935

Tower height: 58 feet

Elevation of the focal
plane: 78 feet

Optic: Modern

Status: Active

Characteristic: Flashes
red every 6 seconds

Range: 7 miles

Position: 43° 23' 10
87° 51' 35

Note: Unusual wishbone
shape

In the eyes of many, the Port Washington North Breakwater tower may appear severely utilitarian, as if designed with no thought whatever to its appearance, but this is not the case. The tower owes its unusual wishbone shape to the modernist architecture of the art deco era. Its architect likely thought it was beautiful, so take a closer look and perhaps you will agree. Built in 1935 atop an open-arch concrete platform, the structure was, at the very least, durable, as it remains an active aid to navigation after more than seventy years of service to mariners. Unlike traditional lighthouses, it has no lantern room. Instead, its automated lighting apparatus sits on a platform at the top of the tower.

TO SEE THE LIGHT: The breakwater light can be seen from the Port Washington waterfront but is best viewed from a boat.

SHEBOYGAN BREAKWATER LIGHT

Built in 1906, Sheboygan's cast-iron breakwater tower originally stood at the end of a pier near the entrance to the harbor. In 1915 it was relocated to the breakwater where it replaced a vulnerable wooden marker that had suffered severe storm damage. The tower lost its lantern in 1950 and, as a result, is not a particularly handsome structure. The automated light shines from a flat platform atop the tower.

TO SEE THE LIGHT: The Sheboygan Breakwater Light can be seen from Deland Park in downtown Sheboygan. The Sheboygan North Point Lighthouse is located nearby at 124 Lighthouse Court. Built in 1839, it once guided vessels to the city's wharves. Its light was deactivated in 1904, and the old lighthouse was sold to private owners for use as a residence. Also known as the Chippewa Lighthouse, it still stands in town between First and Second Streets.

Location: Sheboygan

Established: 1915

Tower height: 50 feet

Elevation of the focal plane: 55 feet

Optic: Modern

Status: Active

Characteristic: Flashes every 4 seconds

Range: 9 miles

Position: 43° 44' 58
87° 41' 34

Note: No lantern

Rick Polad

Piled up like a stack of toy building blocks, Wisconsin's Manitowoc Breakwater Light is no architectural gem. However, the 40-foot tower has served its purpose well for nearly ninety years and still guides vessels in and out of Manitowoc's busy little harbor. The beacon, focused by a fifth-order Fresnel lens, can still be seen flashing out its warning each night.

Built in 1918, near the end of World War I, the existing building replaced a previous tower that had guarded the Manitowoc River entrance since 1895. Among the first active commercial ports on Lake Michigan, Manitowoc had a lighthouse as early as 1840. Today, more than a century and a half later, Manitowoc remains an important destination for Lake Michigan shipping.

For many years Manitowoc's lights guided the ferries that carried railroad cars back and forth across the lake. Some of these stout, workmanlike vessels are still in use, but nowadays they load up with automobiles and passengers rather than boxcars. The ferry trip from Manitowoc to Ludington, Michigan, is an unforgettable experience. The crossing takes up to five hours, and for about half that time, no land can be seen. The ferries are popular with birds as well as people: Gulls may follow one all the way across the lake, a straight-line distance of 60 miles across open water.

TO SEE THE LIGHT: Manitowoc is located just off Interstate 43 and Highway 42 about an hour and a half north of Milwaukee. The lighthouse can be seen from several excellent viewpoints on the Manitowoc waterfront. The closest view is from the marina just off Maritime Drive. The light can also be seen and photographed from the deck of the Manitowoc–Ludington ferry. For ferry information call (800) 841–4243. While in Manitowoc don't miss the Wisconsin Maritime Museum at 75 Maritime Drive; (920) 684–0218; wisconsinmaritime.org. The museum houses several fine Fresnel lenses including a fourth-order lens that once served here.

Location: Manitowoc

Established: 1840

Tower height: 40 feet

Elevation of the focal plane: 52 feet

Optic: Fresnel (fifth order)

Status: Active

Characteristic: 3 seconds on and 3 seconds off

Range: 15 miles

Position: 44° 05' 34
87° 38' 37

Note: Favorite of cross-lake ferry passengers

RAWLEY POINT LIGHT

Location: Two Rivers

Established: 1854

Tower height: 110 feet

Elevation of the focal
plane: 113 feet

Optic: Modern

Status: Active

Characteristic: Flashes
every 15 seconds

Range: 28 miles

Position: 44° 12' 42
87° 30' 30

Note: Ornate, multitiered
lantern

The waters around Rawley Point just north of Two Rivers, Wisconsin, are deceptively tranquil. Not far from shore a deadly shoal lurks just beneath the surface of Lake Michigan, waiting to rip open the hull of any vessel that strays too near. After several tragic nineteenth-century wrecks, a light was finally placed on the point to warn ships against the danger. Completed in 1854, it guided mariners with a modest beacon that beamed from a small tower and lantern perched on the roof of the keeper's dwelling. In 1894 this light was replaced by the soaring metal tower that still guards Rawley Point. More than 110 feet tall, the present tower is a steel-skeleton structure with a central cylinder braced by eight legs. At the top is a three-level lantern complex equipped with an unusually powerful airport-style beacon. Its light can be seen from 28 miles away.

TO SEE THE LIGHT: The tower and adjacent two-and-one-half-story dwelling, now a Coast Guard residence, are closed to the public, but respectful visitors are welcome to walk the grounds. The station is surrounded by lush and beautiful Point Beach State Forest, which offers camping, picnicking, hiking, and a wonderful opportunity to view the lighthouse. From Two Rivers follow County Road O and Sandy Bay Road to Point Beach. For information call (920) 794–7480.

Off Twenty-second and Jackson Streets in Two Rivers is the upper portion of the old Two Rivers Pierhead Lighthouse (1883). It stands adjacent to the Rogers Street Fishing Village Museum; visit www.rogersstreet.com.

The contrast between the old harbor lighthouse at Two Rivers (left) and the soaring steel skeleton tower at Rawley Point could hardly be more profound.

KEWAUNEE PIERHEAD LIGHT

Location: Kewaunee

Established: 1891

Tower height: 43 feet

Elevation of the focal plane: 45 feet

Optic: Fresnel (fifth order)

Status: Active

Characteristic: Fixed white

Range: 15 miles

Position: 44° 27' 30 87° 29' 48

Note: Marks the Kewaunee River entrance

The picturesque town of Kewaunee has been served by a series of navigational lights, the first of them built in 1891. The current Kewaunee light, completed in 1931, shines from a substantial steel-and-concrete structure at the end of the harbor's south pier. It consists of a 43-foot square tower rising from the end of a hefty fog-signal building. The original fifth-order Fresnel lens remains in operation, guiding vessels into the mouth of the Kewaunee River.

This combination tower and fog-signal building is a near twin of "Big Red," a pier light located across the lake at Holland, Michigan. The Kewaunee Pierhead Light is mostly white, however, while the one at Holland is bright red. Built at about the same time, both were designed to house the bulky boilers that drove their powerful fog signals.

TO SEE THE LIGHT: Located at the end of the pier on the north side of the Kewaunee River, entrance Route 42, the lighthouse is closed to the public and is best seen from a boat.

ALGOMA PIERHEAD LIGHT

Location: Algoma

Established: 1908

Tower height: 48 feet

Elevation of the focal plane: 42 feet

Optic: Fresnel (fifth order)

Status: Active

Characteristic: Red interrupted every 6 seconds

Range: 16 miles

Position: 44° 36' 24
87° 25' 48

Note: Stacked towers

Bob and Sandra Shanklin, The Lighthouse People

This rather unusual structure, located at the end of Algoma's north pier, consists of two separate cylindrical steel towers stacked one on top of the other. The upper tower dates to 1908 and served here alone until 1932, when maritime officials concluded that it was too short to adequately mark the Algoma harbor. Rather than pull it down and build a new tower, they brought in a second metal tower and placed the original one on top. The new arrangement more than doubled the elevation of the beacon and significantly increased its range. Still focused by a classic fifth-order Fresnel lens, the light remains in operation.

TO SEE THE LIGHT: The lighthouse stands at the end of the breakwater on the north side of Anahpee River near downtown Algoma.

CHAPTER TWO

DOORWAY TO GREEN BAY: FROM STURGEON BAY TO GREEN BAY

Located on the 100-mile-long peninsula that separates Green Bay from the open waters of Lake Michigan, Wisconsin's scenic Door County is a lighthouse lover's wonderland. In fact, it is home to more historic light towers than any other county in the United States. A glance at a map makes it clear why this long slender county needs so many navigational lights. All lake traffic approaching the bustling port of Green Bay must either take the Sturgeon Bay Ship Canal that cuts through the waist of the county or round the tip of the peninsula some 50 miles to the northeast. In either case ship pilots need plenty of guidance to stay on course and away from the dangerous rocks that litter the rugged shores.

Although it literally serves as the doorway to Green Bay, that is not how Door County got its name. Instead, the name reflects the grim early history of the peninsula. A Native American legend tells of Pottawatomis who lured ashore the canoes of their enemies, the Cape Indians, with a misleading signal fire and then massacred the stranded warriors. For this reason and others, those who brave the stormy waters of Lake Michigan and Green Bay have long known the peninsula as "Death's Door." More than a few ships and sailors would end their days on or near the peninsula's deadly shores. Among these may very well have been the very first European-style trading ship to sail the Great Lakes' wide, open waters.

The "Griffon" at Death's Door

In 1679 the French explorer Sieur de La Salle and a party of fur traders built a fifty-ton sailing ship, pushing her off into Lake Erie from a rough-hewn shipyard near where the city of Buffalo, New York, now stands. This was no crude, overbuilt canoe. Christened the *Griffon*, she was more than 60 feet long and had five cannon arrayed below the deck. La Salle and his fellow adventurers intended to make themselves rich by filling the *Griffon's* holds with muskrat and beaver pelts gathered by French trappers.

The *Griffon* proved a worthy ship, weathering more than one fierce storm on the outbound leg of her maiden voyage to Green Bay and the shores of what is known today as Wisconsin. There the *Griffon's* crew loaded her up with a rich cargo of pelts before setting sail for the east. Having disembarked to continue his explorations—and discover the upper Mississippi River—La Salle watched the *Griffon* disappear over the horizon. He was confident that the ship and her cargo of furs would safely reach their destination and make him a rich man, but it was not to be. Somewhere, perhaps not far off the tip of the Door Peninsula, she was smashed by a sudden, sharp autumn gale. Commercial navigation on the Great Lakes thus got off to an ominous start, and since then thousands of fine ships have been lost on the lakes along with their passengers and crews.

To warn mariners and guide their vessels safely around the peninsula, the government built at least a dozen lighthouses here. Most still stand and more than a few remain in operation. Nowadays sailors are not the only ones interested in these historic towers. Door

The Old Baileys Harbor Lighthouse can be seen from the mainland.

County attracts droves of summertime tourists who enjoy the scenery and the hospitality of pleasant towns such as Sturgeon Bay, Ephraim, and Baileys Harbor, and who visit historic lighthouses.

Cutting through the Fog

Most of the light stations in Door County and along other stretches of Wisconsin lakeshore are equipped with powerful foghorns. Since the Great Lakes' thick fogs make it difficult, if not impossible, to see a lighthouse beacon, sound signals are needed to warn vessels away from prominent headlands or navigational obstacles.

Throughout history a wide array of noise-making devices has been used as fog signals. Some keepers blew trumpets, fired off cannons, or rang heavy bells, but even lowing cattle or barking dogs might alert mariners and help avert disaster. The world's earliest fog signals were probably used in Europe or the Middle East, where drums or bells likely helped mariners find safe harbor or warned them away from rocks. The first fog signal in what would eventually become the United States was a cannon placed at Boston Harbor light in 1719. While cannons could certainly be heard, it was not possible to load and fire them continuously over extended periods. As a result, bells soon replaced cannons as the signal of choice.

At first fog bells had to be struck by hand, but weary keepers soon found ways to make the task less tiring and monotonous. Sometimes they attached a long cord to the clapper and ran it through an opening in the wall of the residence. That way, at least they could be comfortable while ringing the bell.

About the middle of the nineteenth century, fog bells began to be replaced by horns, trumpets, whistles, and sirens, most of them driven by steam. Among the earliest of these was an extraordinary device invented by C. L. Daboll during the 1850s. It directed compressed air or steam from a boiler over a reed, filling a large trumpet with sound. Some of Daboll's trumpets were enormous, measuring up to 17 feet in length and as much as 3 feet in width at the opening.

The Daboll trumpet was never widely used, but similar sound signals became common, and steam whistles or pump-driven horns could be heard along foggy coastlines everywhere. Some had a double-tone, or diaphone, signal, a system invented in Canada. The moaning of diaphone foghorns was once familiar to inhabitants of

coastal communities everywhere. Many claimed to enjoy their calls—
often deep-throated and sonorous—but others found them annoying.
Some foghorn signals have been compared to the "protests of a
wounded moose" or the "complaints of a cow that needs milking."

The U.S. Coast Guard has standardized the electrically
powered, pump-driven horns it now uses
to warn mariners. They come in three
sizes with ranges of 1 to 5 miles. These
sound signals are turned on and off auto-
matically by monitors that measure the
level of moisture in the air with strobe
lights and photoelectric sensors.

Usually, fog signals and the equipment required to produce them are
housed in separate wooden, concrete, or
cast-iron buildings. Some fog-signal buildings double as platforms for navigational
lights. Several Wisconsin navigational
stations feature combined light-and-fog-
signal structures.

When steam-powered horns were
introduced during the latter half of the
nineteenth century, fog-signal buildings
became far more substantial structures.
Sometimes nearly as large as the station
residence, they housed an impressive
array of boilers, wheels, pulleys, horns,
and whistles, all of which made them look
like small factories. A large supply of coal
had to be kept on hand either in the fog-
signal building itself or in a nearby
storage building.

A summertime flowerbox
adds a splash of color to
the Cana Island
Lighthouse in Door
County.

During the twentieth century electric foghorns replaced steam-
driven devices, and sizable buildings were no longer needed to
house the fog-signal equipment. Even so, many fog-signal buildings
were left standing for use as workrooms, storehouses, or garages.
Nowadays, with the growth in popularity of light stations as tourist
attractions, a few old fog-signal buildings have been pressed into
service as museum display spaces or even gift shops.

STURGEON BAY SHIP CANAL LIGHT

A tour of Door County lighthouses might well begin with the 98-foot skeleton tower of the Sturgeon Bay Ship Canal Lighthouse, which features a powerful third-order Fresnel lens. The tower seen here today dates from 1903 but is not the original; it doesn't even look like the tower erected near the entrance to the canal four years earlier. The earlier structure had been designed by Lighthouse Service engineers as an experiment. Completed in 1899, it consisted of a pencil-shaped steel cylinder held erect by latticework buttresses, which, as it turned out, proved unequal to the strong winds that frequently howled in off Lake Michigan. The addition of guy wires failed to dampen wind-related vibrations that were so violent they knocked the station's lens off its mount. Eventually, the tower had to be supported by an outer hexagonal steel skeleton, and as a result, the existing structure is essentially a lighthouse within a lighthouse.

This unusual sentinel was originally one of several marking the eastern portal of a canal linking Lake Michigan with Green Bay. Built by the Sturgeon Bay and Lake Michigan Canal and Harbor Company as a profit-making venture, the canal provided freighters with a welcome shortcut to the bustling wharves at Green Bay. Completed in 1882, the canal remained in private hands until 1893 when it was purchased by the government and turned over to the U.S. Corps of Engineers.

TO SEE THE LIGHT: Located near the Bay View Bridge off Lake Forest Road, the lighthouse is part of an active Coast Guard station and is closed to the public except during an annual Door County Lighthouse Walk. For information on this annual event, call the Door County Maritime Museum at (920) 743–5958 or visit www.dcmm.org. However, the tower can be photographed and enjoyed from a nearby pier.

Location: Sturgeon Bay

Established: 1899

Tower height: 98 feet

Elevation of the focal plane: 107 feet

Optic: Fresnel (third order)

Status: Active

Characteristic: Flashes red every 10 seconds

Range: 17 miles

Position: 44° 47' 42 87° 18' 48

Note: Marks the entrance to a strategic canal

STURGEON BAY SHIP CANAL NORTH PIERHEAD LIGHT

Consisting of a substantial fog-signal building with attached tower, this lighthouse is similar to a number of other Great Lakes pierhead sentinels, including the famous Holland Harbor ("Big Red") Light across the lake in Michigan. Like the latter structure, this one is painted bright red.

The station derives its rather long and clumsy name from the ship canal that cuts through the Door Peninsula. The canal links Green Bay to the open waters of Lake Michigan and saves time and money for shipping interests serving Green Bay. The lighthouse marks the Lake Michigan entrance to the canal. A metal catwalk provides access to the tower when high waves make walking the stone pier too dangerous.

TO SEE THE LIGHT: Both this lighthouse and the nearby Sturgeon Bay Ship Canal Light are located near the Bay View Bridge off Lake Forest Road. With its metal catwalk, octagonal lantern, and striking red roof, the pierhead tower can be seen and enjoyed either from the pier itself or from Portage Park in Sturgeon Bay. To reach the pier, follow Canal Drive to Lake Forest Park Road and park near the Coast Guard station entrance.

An elevated walkway allowed keepers to reach the offshore Sturgeon Bay Ship Canal North Pierhead tower even in a raging Lake Michigan storm. Nowadays the light is automated.

Location: Sturgeon Bay

Established: 1903

Tower height: 39 feet

Elevation of the focal plane: 40 feet

Optic: Modern

Status: Active

Characteristic: Flashes red every 2.5 seconds

Range: 9 miles

Position: 44° 47' 30
87° 18' 36

Note: Serves as a range light

BAILEYS HARBOR RANGE LIGHTHOUSES

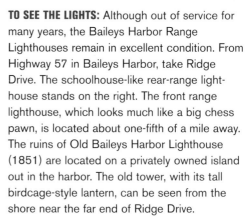

Location: Baileys Harbor

Established: 1870

Tower height: 35 feet (rear)

Elevation of the focal plane: 39 feet (rear)

Optic: Fresnel (inactive)

Status: Decommissioned in 1969

Note: Handsomely maintained historic range-light station

To guide ships along the stretch of Lake Michigan nearest to Baileys Harbor, the Lighthouse Board established a pair of range lights here in 1870. These lights replaced a much older, single-lens lighthouse located on a small island far out in the harbor (see page 35). Range lights mark shipping channels by displaying not one but at least two lights, arrayed one behind the other. When viewed from midchannel, the lights appear one atop the other and perpendicular to the surface of the water. If the lights begin to tilt to the right or left, a pilot knows that his ship may be straying dangerously out of the channel.

At Baileys Harbor the lower, or front-range, light was housed in a squat, 21-foot wooden tower down beside the lake. The upper, or rear-range, light shined from a gabled tower atop a clapboard dwelling some 1,000 feet inland. The station was automated in 1930 and afterward was cared for by Lutheran ministers, who used the dwelling as a parsonage right up until the lights were discontinued during the 1960s.

TO SEE THE LIGHTS: Although out of service for many years, the Baileys Harbor Range Lighthouses remain in excellent condition. From Highway 57 in Baileys Harbor, take Ridge Drive. The schoolhouse-like rear-range lighthouse stands on the right. The front range lighthouse, which looks much like a big chess pawn, is located about one-fifth of a mile away. The ruins of Old Baileys Harbor Lighthouse (1851) are located on a privately owned island out in the harbor. The old tower, with its tall birdcage-style lantern, can be seen from the shore near the far end of Ridge Drive.

With its steeplelike tower, the Baileys Harbor Rear Range Lighthouse (right) looks a bit like a country church, while its front-range neighbor (left) resembles a chess piece. The two lights were displayed in tandem to keep vessels safely within the harbor approach channel.

THE ARCHITECTURE–AND POLITICS– OF LIGHT

The business end of a lighthouse is, of course, at the top. The lighting apparatus is placed in the lantern room as high above sea level as possible. Height adds to the beacon's range, or distance from which it can be seen. But equally important to the beacon's effectiveness is the strength of the light itself. Usually a lens, mirror, or other optical device is used to concentrate the light, often into a single brilliant flash. For many years, the most efficient way of doing this was with a Fresnel lens.

Invented in 1822 by French physicist Augustin-Jean Fresnel, these big prismatic glass lenses were designed to snatch every flicker of light from even the smallest lamp and concentrate it into a powerful beam that could be seen from dozens of miles away. Fresnel's elegant lenses did their job so well that they soon became standard equipment in lighthouses throughout much of the world.

However, the new Fresnel technology was virtually ignored for decades in the United States, where Winslow Lewis's far less effective parabolic reflectors were employed until the mid-nineteenth century. One reason the United States was slow to adopt the Fresnel system was the considerable expense of importing the lenses from France. Another was the bureaucratic fussiness of Stephen Pleasonton, the U.S. Treasury auditor who served for many years as head of the nation's lighthouse system. Displaying undisguised favoritism for Lewis, a personal friend, Pleasonton continued to equip U.S. lighthouses with his outdated reflectors, even though they were demon-

This third-order Fresnel lens on Devils Island was manufactured in the late nineteenth century.

strably inferior to Fresnel lenses. Following the release of a highly critical report written by Lewis's own nephew, Pleasonton was forced into retirement.

In 1852 stewardship of America's navigational lights passed to a Lighthouse Board consisting of military officers, engineers, harbor masters, and experienced seamen. The board immediately under-took a complete overhaul of America's ill-equipped and, in many cases, sadly neglected lighthouses. As part of this effort, most light-houses were fitted with sparkling new Fresnel lenses.

Remarkably, Fresnel lenses are as effective and useful today as they were 150 years ago. This is a claim that can be made for very few devices. Long before the development of space rockets, jet airliners, automobiles, or even side-wheel steamships, Fresnel lenses were already shining in lighthouse towers. To fully appreciate the contrast, consider that some early Fresnels were delivered in horse-drawn carts to the light stations where they were to serve.

Fresnels come in a variety of sizes, referred to as "orders." The huge first-order lenses are 6 feet or more in diameter and up to 12 feet tall. The smallest lenses, designated sixth-order, are only about 1 foot in diameter and not much larger than a gallon jug. The larger and more powerful first-, second-, and third-order lenses were intended for use in coastal lighthouses. The smaller fourth-, fifth-, and sixth-order lenses saw use mostly in harbor and river lighthouses.

At one time nearly all of Wisconsin's lighthouses were equipped with Fresnel lenses. While no less effective than modern lighthouse optical devices, these beautiful lenses require considerable care and must be cleaned and polished frequently by hand. Each lens consists of individual prisms—sometimes more than a thousand—fitted into a metal frame. This makes them look like giant glass beehives; it also makes them rather delicate. So the Coast Guard has removed them from most lighthouses and replaced them with plastic lenses or airport-type beacons. Many of the old lenses are on exhibit in museums, such as the National Lakeshore Visitor Center in Bayfield in the Apostle Islands. But original Fresnel lenses remain in a few lighthouses in the Great Lakes. In Wisconsin the Devils Island Station retains its beautiful classic lens.

During the nineteenth century, Fresnel lenses were hand ground and hand polished by the poorest classes of French laborers, who often worked for pennies a day. It is ironic that the handiwork of these unremembered workers can be counted among the most practical, durable, and handsome devices ever made. No one will ever know how many lives have been saved by these fine old lenses or how many accidents were avoided because their guiding light could be seen on the horizon.

The LaPointe Light uses a modern optic, as do most of today's lighthouses.

CANA ISLAND LIGHT

An aerial view of Cana
Island shows the light-
house at the end opposite
the causeway.

On a clear night the impressive Cana Island Light throws its beam 17 miles out into Lake Michigan. Established in 1870, the light marks the northern approaches to Baileys Harbor. To make sure that the 86-foot tower and adjacent one-and-a-half-story dwelling could withstand the lake's prodigious storms, construction crews built the structures with brick, in this case a light-colored variety. But just as a yellow-brick road may lead to an uncertain future, so too with yellow-brick light-houses. Within just a few decades, the brick showed signs of severe weathering and the tower seemed in danger of crumbling. To protect it, the Lighthouse Board had the tower encased in a cocoonlike shell made of individual metal plates riveted together. A low, white-stone causeway connects Cana Island to the mainland.

TO SEE THE LIGHT: To get to Cana Island Light, take Highway 57 north out of Baileys Harbor. After about 1 mile turn right onto County Road G, go 4 more miles, and turn right onto Route 38 (Cana Island Road). Follow this rustic but paved road to the end. To reach the lighthouse, you must park and walk across a causeway covered by about 10 inches of water. The tower and keeper's home are not open to the public, but the view is worth getting your feet wet. The Door County Maritime Museum leases the station from the U.S. Coast Guard, and it is open to the public daily. Call (920) 743–5958 or call the chamber of commerce at (800) 527–3529.

Location: Cana Island
near Baileys Harbor

Established: 1870

Tower height: 86 feet

Elevation of the focal
plane: 89 feet

Optic: Fresnel
(third order)

Status: Active

Characteristic: Fixed
white

Range: 17 miles

Position: 45° 05' 18
87° 02' 48

Note: Unusually beautiful
lighthouse

POTTAWATOMIE LIGHT (ROCK ISLAND)

📷 🎦 🚗

Location: Gills Rock in
Green Bay

Established: 1836

Tower height: 41 feet

Elevation of the focal
plane: 159 feet

Optic: Modern

Status: Active

Characteristic: Flashes
every 4 seconds

Range: 7 miles

Position 45° 25' 42
86° 49' 42

Note: Light was recently
reactivated

A chain of rock-strewn islands forms an extension of the long, daggerlike peninsula that forms Door County. The jagged shores of these islands and the shoals that lie between them have claimed countless vessels. To guide ships safely around these formidable obstacles, the government established on Rock Island, at the end of the chain, one of the first light stations in the western Great Lakes. Completed in 1836, the original Pottawatomie Lighthouse—named for a local Indian tribe—served until 1858, when a hurricane-like storm swept it into the lake. Given massive walls of stone, the combination keeper's residence and light tower that replaced it still stands. Unfortunately, the lantern was removed after the station was discontinued during the 1920s, but in 1999 Wisconsin preservationists restored the lantern, and the light itself was recently reactivated.

TO SEE THE LIGHTS: The lighthouse is located in Wisconsin's Rock Island State Park. Visitors must take a ferry from Northport, at the northern end of Highway 42, to Washington Island and then a second ferry to Rock Island. Contact Washington Island Ferry, Washington Island, WI 54246; (920) 847–2546 or (800) 223–2094. The ferry provides excellent views of the Plum Island Range Lighthouse (1897), a white skeleton tower, and the Pilot Island Lighthouse (1858), a historic brick combination tower and dwelling. Occasional tours of the Pottawatomie Light are offered by the Friends of Rock Island; www.wctc.net/~cmarlspc.

The **Plum Island Lighthouse** dates to the late nineteenth century. Its keeper's house and still operational skeleton-tower light can be seen from ferries approaching nearby Pottawatomie Island.

Intricate details add
architectural appeal to
America's historic
lighthouses.

Marking a safe channel from Lake Michigan into Green Bay, the Eagle Bluff Light first shined in 1868, the same year that Ulysses S. Grant was elected president. Its square, 43-foot brick tower was set at a diagonal into the side of the one-and-a-half-story dwelling. This made it easier for keepers to reach the tower—and keep warm—when cold winds blew in off the lake. Ironically, there has been no keeper here since the station was automated in 1926. The Eagle Bluff Light was among the first in America to operate without a full-time keeper. Still active, the old lighthouse has done its work alone for more than eighty years.

The attractive brick keeper's dwelling has been beautifully restored. The Door County Historical Society maintains a museum in the dwelling as one of the many attractions of Peninsula State Park, which also offers hiking, fishing, swimming, and golf.

TO SEE THE LIGHT: Follow Highway 42 to Fish Creek and the entrance to Peninsula State Park. Once inside the park, follow Shore Drive for about 4 miles to the lighthouse; call the Door County Historical Society at (920) 839–2377. Several miles to the west is the boarded-up Chambers Island Lighthouse (1868).

Location: Ephraim

Established: 1868

Tower height: 43 feet

Elevation of the focal plane: 75 feet

Optic: Fresnel (fifth order)

Status: Active

Characteristic: Flashes every 6 seconds

Range: 7 miles

Position: 45° 10' 06 87° 14' 12

Note: Museum in keeper's residence

CHAMBERS ISLAND LIGHT

During the middle of the nineteenth century, sawmills along Green Bay hummed around the clock, processing the prodigious bounty of Wisconsin's vast forests. Nearly all of the lumber produced in this region of Wisconsin was loaded onto freighters and shipped through the bay and the mighty chain of lakes beyond to markets in the east. Freighters—bound for bustling lumber ports such as Ephraim, Sturgeon Bay, and the town of

Bob and Sandra Shanklin,
The Lighthouse People

Green Bay—first rounded the Door Peninsula and then turned toward the southwest, where they soon encountered a broad, rocky island lying squarely astride the shipping lanes. To guide them around the island, the government established a lighthouse here in 1868.

A near twin of the Eagle Bluff Light, also built at about this time, the Chambers Island light station consisted of an octagonal tower attached to a one-and-a-half-story keeper's residence. Both structures were built with yellow brick. Lewis Williams was named the station's first keeper, apparently in return for selling the land needed for the lighthouse. Lewis remained the keeper for more than twenty years, but at least seven other keepers would follow in his footsteps. In 1961 the station lost both its keeper and its light when the old lighthouse was boarded up and a utilitarian steel-skeleton light tower was built nearby. Fitted with a modern, automated optic, the steel tower still guides mariners. The old lighthouse now serves as an attraction of Chambers Island Park.

Location: Chambers Island near Fish Creek
Established: 1868
Tower height: 67 feet
Elevation of the focal plane: 68 feet
Optic: Modern (steel tower)
Status: Active
Characteristic: Flashes every 6 seconds
Range: 10 miles
Position: 45° 12' 06 87° 21' 54
Note: Near twin of the nearby Eagle Bluff Light

TO SEE THE LIGHT: The lighthouse is open to the public on weekends during warm-weather months. The island must be reached by water. The Door County Maritime Museum in Sturgeon Bay offers occasional tours; call (920) 743–5958.

Although the Chambers
Island Lighthouse long
ago lost its lantern, a
nearby skeleton tower
still displays the station's
beacon.

Bob and Sandra Shanklin,

The Lighthouse People

SHERWOOD POINT LIGHT

Location: Near Sturgeon Bay

Established: 1883

Tower height: 37 feet

Elevation of the focal plane: 61 feet

Optic: Modern

Status: Active

Characteristic: 3 seconds on, 3 seconds off

Range: 15 miles

Position: 44° 53' 36 87° 26' 00

Note: The last Great Lakes lighthouse to be automated (1983)

Completed in 1883, the square, 37-foot brick tower is attached to the front of the keeper's residence. Although the Coast Guard still uses the handsome, though small, keeper's dwelling as a residence, the light is automated. This was the last lighthouse on the Great Lakes with a full-time staff, and it was not automated until 1983. Ironically, the Eagle Bluff Light a couple of dozen miles to the northeast was among the first to be automated. The Sherwood Point station retained its fourth-order Fresnel lens until 2002 (as shown in the photo below), but a modern optic now produces its beacon. A small, pyramidal fog-signal building stands near the tower.

TO SEE THE LIGHT: As part of an active Coast Guard station, the lighthouse is off-limits to the public. It is best viewed from the water. Standing atop a massive caisson on the other side of Green Bay is the open-water Peshtigo Reef Light.

The Sherwood Point Light is pictured here with its fourth-order Fresnel lens in place. The lens has since been replaced by a modern optic.

PESHTIGO REEF LIGHT

Location: Green Bay

Established: 1934

Tower height: 72 feet

Elevation of the focal
plane: 72 feet

Optic: Modern

Status: Active

Characteristic: Flashes
every 6 seconds

Range: 9 miles

Position: 44° 57' 24
87° 34' 48

Note: Built on an
open-water crib

During ancient times the Romans used the hulk of an enormous Egyptian freighter, said to have belonged to Cleopatra, as a makeshift foundation for the Ostia Lighthouse a few miles from their imperial capital. To stabilize the foundation, builders used the big ship as a "crib," filling it with rocks and rubble. Some 2,000 years later American lighthouse builders also made extensive use of cribs, especially in the Great Lakes, but their methods were some- what less showy. To provide an adequate if not rock-solid foundation, they assembled wooden cribs on land and then towed them to the construction site, where they were filled with broken stone and chunks of concrete. Having settled securely on the bottom, the crib was capped with concrete and a tower was erected on top.

Rising more than 70 feet above the waters of Green Bay, the Peshtigo Reef Light stands on a substantial crib foundation placed

here in 1934. The crib and steel- cylinder light tower it supports have survived countless Great Lakes storms. The light still func- tions, warning mariners away from an obstacle once known as Whale- back Shoal because of its humped, whalelike shape.

TO SEE THE LIGHT:
Closed to the public, the Peshtigo Reef Light is accessible only by boat.

Bob and Sandra Shanklin,
The Lighthouse People

Like the Baileys Harbor Range Lights and similar double-light beacons throughout the Great Lakes, Green Bay's Grassy Island Range Lights were intended to help navigators keep their vessels within a narrow safe channel. Also like the range lights at Baileys Harbor, these are no longer functional. In fact, they were moved from their original locations near the entrance to Green Bay harbor when the station was deactivated in 1966. The old towers now stand on the grounds of the Green Bay Yacht Club, where they are under restoration by volunteers.

TO SEE THE LIGHTS: Currently, the club and its lighthouses are not open to the public.

Location: Green Bay

Established: 1872

Tower height: 36 feet (rear), 26 feet (front)

Status: Deactivated in 1966

Note: Owned by a yacht club

CHAPTER THREE

LIGHTS OF THE APOSTLES: FROM MICHIGAN ISLAND TO SAND ISLAND

Lake Superior is a mammoth body of water more than 350 miles from end to end. Early pioneers and lake sailors were amazed by its sheer size and by the terrifying storms that often raged over its surface. For much of the nineteenth century, the lake remained a frontier with only the tiniest settlements dotting its shores. In many ways it is still a frontier, and visitors gazing out over its waters cannot help feeling a certain awe and desolation. They cannot help asking themselves how a fresh-water lake could be so enormous. Mariners, on the other hand, wonder why it is so deadly. Several thousand ships, including the fabled *Edmund Fitzgerald,* have been lost in its depths.

Dozens of grand navigational lights ring the big lake. The Apostle Islands National Lakeshore, just off the Wisconsin mainland, can boast no fewer than seven historic lighthouses, some dating to before the Civil War and most still active. Easily accessible to visitors in summer, this well-preserved collection makes the Apostles a lighthouse lover's paradise—what travel writers have in fact described as a veritable "lighthouse national park."

As anyone who has seen them is likely to agree, the islands, located off Wisconsin's Chequamegon Peninsula, are truly a national treasure. Fortunately, Congress has recognized their unique aesthetic value and has set aside twenty-one of the twenty-two islands by making them part of the Apostle Islands National Lakeshore.

Every summer the islands attract more and more visitors, who flock here to enjoy their natural beauty, wildlife, and pristine beaches. But the islands offer another extraordinary attraction as well: Strung in a semicircle around the island chain is an elegant jeweled necklace of six lighthouses, all of them more than a century old and all in excellent condition.

Not long after the Sand Island Lighthouse went into service in 1881, its keeper was involved in a daring rescue. The following quote from the September 19, 1885, edition of the *Bayfield County* (Wisconsin) *Press* tells the story:

Saturday morning of last week Lighthouse keeper Lederle of
Sand Island Light discovered a large boat on fire about ten
miles off that point. He immediately launched his boat and,
notwithstanding the fact that it was blowing almost a gale
from the southeast, set out for the burning steamer. When out
several miles, he passed the captain, mate, engineer, and
fireman of the ill-fated craft, who were pulling for shore in a
metallic lifeboat. They informed him that the steamer had been
abandoned and that the remainder of her crew, six men and
one woman, were in a yawl boat and were being carried out
into the lake. Mr. Lederle kept on his course and in a short
time overhauled the yawl boat, the crew of which had given

Resembling the shell of a
chambered nautilus, a
spiral staircase winds
upward through the
Michigan Island tower.

up all hope of reaching land, owing to the heavy sea and high wind which prevailed. They were soon transferred to the light-house boat and safely conveyed to shore, picking up on the return trip the occupants of the lifeboat.

The greatest danger facing mariners navigating the southern reaches of Lake Superior has never been fire or even storm, but the Apostles themselves. The islands jut out into the lake like sharp knives waiting to slash the hulls of vessels that stray too near. No doubt countless ships and lives have been saved by the lights that ring the island chain. For nearly a century these important beacons were focused by Fresnel lenses. These sparkling prismatic lenses were once considered marvels of science, and anyone lucky enough to see one of these beautiful polished-glass optics nowadays will likely still consider it marvelous.

Saving the Lights

Even when brightened by Fresnel lenses or suitable modern substitutes, lighthouse beacons cannot make Wisconsin's lakeshores or any coastline totally safe for navigation. With its confusion of fog-shrouded channels and headlands, the Apostle Islands in particular remain a dangerous place for ships. Fortunately, nowadays mariners can rely on a mind-boggling array of sophisticated electronic devices that make navigation easier and much safer. The satellite driven Global Positioning System (GPS) can tell a navigator precisely where a vessel is and where it is headed. But when they need a visual reference or on those rare occasions when their shipboard electronics fail, seamen are always happy to see a guiding light on the horizon. For this reason and others, the Coast Guard continues to operate major shore lights, such as those in the Apostles, but the lighthouses themselves are, perhaps by necessity, considered of lesser importance.

No longer cared for by resident keepers, many of America's historic light towers have begun to deteriorate. For some the damage may be irreversible. Happily, it seems that lighthouses have far more friends than anyone thought. Intent on preserving old light towers and other reminders of our nation's rich maritime heritage, local, regional, and national lighthouse organizations have sprung up and are attracting new members every day.

It would seem that Wisconsin, in particular, is well populated with lighthouse lovers, and lighthouses here may be among the best cared for in the nation. While most of the state's lighthouses are now looked after by local governments or private groups, those in the Apostles have been placed in the care of the National Park Service. Visitors are likely to agree that the NPS has been a good steward.

From their ships, seamen are able to view the full extent of the Outer Island Light tower.

MICHIGAN ISLAND LIGHT

📟 🚪 🖼 📷

Location: Apostle Islands

Established: 1857

Tower height: 118 feet

Elevation of the focal
plane: 170 feet

Optic: Modern

Status: Active (old lighthouse deactivated
in 1929)

Characteristic: Flashes
every 6 seconds

Range: 11 miles

Position: 46° 52' 18
90° 29' 48

Note: Oldest Wisconsin
light station on Lake
Superior

Built in 1857, the Michigan Island Lighthouse is the oldest of the seven lighthouses in the Apostle Islands. The original is shown on page 64. During the late 1920s mariners requested a more powerful light be placed in this part of the Apostles, and that required a taller tower. Rather than raise the height of the existing tower, the Lighthouse Service had a steel-skeleton tower moved here from the East Coast. Consisting of an enclosed central steel cylinder braced by six legs, the 118-foot structure had stood at Schooner Ledge on the Delaware River in Pennsylvania. Placed in service in 1930, the New Michigan Island Light remains active and can be seen from up to 11 miles out in Lake Superior.

TO SEE THE LIGHT: The Michigan Island Lighthouses are located in the Apostle Islands National Lakeshore. Visitors must make their own arrangements to get here or to any of the other islands. For information contact the Apostle Islands Cruise Service, P.O. Box 691, City Dock, Bayfield, WI 54814; (715) 779–3925 or (800) 323–7619. During warm-weather months volunteers provide free access to the old lighthouse. Visitors may walk the grounds of the new lighthouse, but they are not allowed to climb the tower.

THE ORIGINAL MICHIGAN ISLAND LIGHTHOUSE

Interestingly, this lighthouse was not used for nearly a dozen years after it was completed, for no sooner had its last stones been laid than it was discovered the light station had been put in the wrong place. Its light had been meant to shine from LaPointe on Long Island well to the south and closer to the Wisconsin mainland. Made aware of the snafu, perhaps by a very embarrassed local official or contractor, federal maritime authorities ordered construction of a second lighthouse on the proper site. In 1869 the Michigan Island Lighthouse was finally placed in operation, and it remained so for more than sixty years, when it was replaced by the steel tower shown on pages 62 and 63.

The original Michigan Island Lighthouse was constructed not long after the Soo Locks opened Lake Superior to shipping from the other lakes. The whitewashed tower and dwelling, with pitched roof and dormers, give this station the look of a New England lighthouse.

LAPOINTE LIGHT

Wisconsin's Madeline Island, which stretches along the south-eastern side of the Apostles chain, was once a thriving fur-trading center. The island attracted throngs of canoes paddled here by trappers, as well as freighters that filled their holds with valuable pelts. To guide vessels around the dangerous southern tip of the island, federal maritime officials decided to build a lighthouse on nearby Long Island. For reasons that have never been clear, the contractors built the lighthouse on Michigan Island instead. Once the mistake became apparent, officials commissioned a second lighthouse to be built in the correct location. Completed in 1858, the wood-frame LaPointe Lighthouse served until 1895, when it was replaced by a steel-skeleton tower similar to the one on Michigan Island.

TO SEE THE LIGHTS: Visitors should stop first at the lakeshore headquarters, located in the Old Courthouse in Bayfield, Wisconsin. Write to Apostle Islands Lakeshore, Chief of Interpretation, Route 1, P.O. Box 4, Bayfield, WI 54814; (715) 779–3398. Boat trips leave Bayfield every day from Memorial Day through mid-October. Private cruises offer trips to each of the most popular islands including Madeline and nearby Long Island, and these provide close-up views of the lighthouses either on land or from the water. For additional information call (800) 323–7619. During the fall the Apostle Islands Lighthouse Celebration features three weeks of special lighthouse cruises and tours.

Location: Apostle Islands
Established: 1858
Tower height: 65 feet
Elevation of the focal plane: 70 feet
Optic: Modern
Status: Active
Characteristic: Green interrupted every 6 seconds
Range: 8 miles
Position: 46° 43' 42
90° 47' 06
Note: Original 1858 tower in ruins

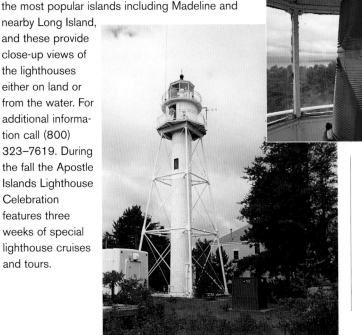

LIGHTHOUSE TRAMWAYS

Some light stations were equipped with tramways to make it easier to move goods from the harbor up to the lighthouse site. A light rail line linking the dock with the station made it possible to load supplies onto small wheeled carts and move them to storage areas with relative ease.

Lighthouse tenders brought foodstuffs and supplies to the island lighthouses sometimes only once every few months. Because they were so infrequent, the deliveries often consisted of large amounts of oil, coal, food, and other necessaries. Sailors either brought the goods ashore in small boats or, when the tender could move in close, offloaded them directly onto the station dock.

Trams, like this one at Outer Island, lifted oil, food, and other supplies up steep embankments to the lighthouse site.

Without a tramway, the keeper and others at the station were forced to lug heavy boxes and barrels to storage areas. More often than not light stations were located a considerable distance above the water, making the job even more strenuous. Having a tramway, as at some of the Apostle Island lighthouses, was a wonderful convenience. In many cases the tramway was built before the lighthouse itself. This simplified the process of bringing in construction materials and equipment.

Powered by a winch, the Michigan Island tram moved supplies from a loading dock on Lake Superior to the station's storage building.

OUTER ISLAND LIGHT

📠 🚹 🏝 📷

Location: Apostle Islands

Established: 1874

Tower height: 80 feet

Elevation of the focal
plane: 129 feet

Optic: Modern
(solar powered)

Status: Active

Characteristic: Flashes
every 10 seconds

Range: 15 miles

Position: 47° 04' 36
90° 25' 00

Note: Soaring white-
brick tower

Ships taking the southern route through Lake Superior must either work their way through the obstacle course thrown in their path by the Apostle Islands or avoid the hazardous channels between the islands by swinging completely around the chain. For more than 130 years, ships have been guided around the Apostles by the Outer Island Light, in service since 1874. A traditional conical brick tower some 80 feet tall, it stands on a high bank, raising the focal plane of its light nearly 130 feet above the lake's surface. The lantern once held a third-order Fresnel lens, but nowadays it employs a plastic lens displaying a flashing white light.

Although automated in 1961, the station was home to keepers and, more often than not, their families as well for more than eighty years. Supplies were brought to the remote islands by specially designed freighters known as tenders. Throughout its history the U.S. Lighthouse Service maintained a sizable fleet of tenders. During the nineteenth century these vessels were often sail powered, but later, steam- and diesel-powered ships took their

place. Many Lighthouse Service tenders were named after flowers, fruits, or trees. For instance, the *Amaranth, Marigold, Orchid, Azalea,* and *Spruce* serviced light stations in the eastern United States and on the Great Lakes. The Coast Guard later continued this tradition, launching tenders such as the *Mistletoe, Sweetgum, Sweetbrier, Red Birch,* and *Papaw.* The tender that most often serviced the Outer Island station was the *Amaranth,* which operated out of Milwaukee and Chicago.

TO SEE THE LIGHT: Visitors should stop first at the lakeshore headquarters, located in the Old Courthouse in Bayfield, Wisconsin. Write to Apostle Islands National Lakeshore, Chief of Interpretation, Route 1, P.O. Box 4, Bayfield, WI 54814; (715) 779–3398; www.nps.gov/apis. Island cruises are available during warm-weather months; call (715) 779–3925 or (800) 323–7619. Vendors offer summertime cruises that pass several of the lights, including the one on Outer Island.

The devil-red cliffs of Devil's Island wait to crush the hulls of misguided vessels. The light-house can be seen in the mist in the upper left corner of the picture.

DEVILS ISLAND LIGHT

*S*o named because of the fiery appearance of its red-rock cliffs, Devils Island stands at the outer, northwestern edge of the Apostle Islands chain. Its strategic position makes it a key turning point for vessels moving along the southern shores of Lake Superior, for it is here that navigators must decide to either plunge into the mazelike Apostles or steer to the north and east and avoid the islands altogether. To help them plot a course and avoid the island's devilish cliffs, the Lighthouse Service placed a navigational station here in 1891. The station's original wooden tower served for only a few years, and in 1898 it was replaced by the existing skeleton structure made of cast iron. Keepers served at this remote station for the better part of a century, and the light was not automated until 1978.

TO SEE THE LIGHT: Guided tours of the Devils Island lighthouse are available during the summer; call (715) 779–3398. All visitors to Devils Island and other Apostle Islands destinations should stop first at the lakeshore headquarters, located in the Old Courthouse in Bayfield, Wisconsin. Write to Apostle Islands National Lakeshore, Chief of Interpretation, Route 1, P.O. Box 4, Bayfield, WI 54814; (715) 779–3398; www.nps.gov/apis. A variety of island cruises is available when weather permits; call (715) 779–3925 or (800) 323–7619.

Location: Apostle Islands

Established: 1891

Tower height: 71 feet

Elevation of the focal plane: 100 feet

Optic: Fresnel (third order)

Status: Active

Characteristic: Flashes red every 10 seconds

Range: 13 miles

Position: 47° 04' 48
90° 43' 42

Note: Pyramidal cast-iron tower

RASPBERRY ISLAND LIGHT

Location: Apostle Islands

Established: 1863

Tower height: 40 feet
(historic tower)

Elevation of the focal
plane: 58 feet (pole light)

Optic: Modern (on pole)

Status: Active (nearby
pole light)

Characteristic: Flashes
every 2.5 seconds
(pole light)

Range: 7 miles (pole
light)

Position: 46° 58' 18
90° 48' 18

Note: Living-history
demonstrations

Located little more than a mile off the mainland, Raspberry Island is relatively easy to reach, and not surprisingly, its lighthouse is the most heavily visited light station in the Apostles. Lighthouse lovers get a real treat here during the summer, when National Lakeshore personnel put on keepers' uniforms and perform living-history demonstrations. The lighthouse has plenty of history, though, unfortunately, no light to offer. Built on a high bank during the Civil War, the lighthouse remained in service for nearly a century, its fifth-order light shining out over the waters of Lake Superior from the lantern room atop its 40-foot tower. The wooden-frame tower and keeper's dwelling still stand, but its light was snuffed out half a

century ago when the Coast Guard replaced it with an automated beacon mounted on a pole in front of the fog-signal building. The old lighthouse is being restored and is otherwise well maintained but even so may not survive for long. The rapidly eroding island cliffs are threatening to pitch the venerable building into the lake.

TO SEE THE LIGHT:

Water taxis, cruises, and special tours are available during the summer. The Apostle Islands Cruise Service offers a variety of interesting excursions—call (715) 779–3925 or (800) 323–7619—and most provide views of the Apostles' historic lighthouses. Nearly all these outings include a stop at Raspberry Island. For fares and schedules, check with the Apostle Islands National Lakeshore in Bayfield; (715) 779–3398; www.nps.gov/apis.

SAND ISLAND LIGHT

Michigan Island 75
to Sand Island

T he westernmost of the light stations in the Apostles, Sand
Island Lighthouse guided ships for half a century—from 1881 to
1931—before its navigational duties were taken over by a light
placed in a nearby steel-skeleton tower. During the next half
century, the old brownstone lighthouse was used as a private residence, but its lantern would not remain dark forever. In 1980 the
Coast Guard restored its beacon and returned the lighthouse to
service.

Today's light is automated and requires only occasional visits
from Coast Guard maintenance personnel, but during its early years
keepers lived at the station year-round. The work here was hard
and demanded an extraordinary variety of skills—even the ability to
handle a dog team. The winter of 1924–25 closed in so fast that a
gas-powered buoy had to be abandoned in Chequamegon Bay,
just east of the Apostles. Before leaving his station for the season,
a keeper drove a dogsled out over the solidly frozen lake, shut off
the gas, and retrieved the buoy's valuable lantern.

Location: Apostle Islands

Established: 1881

Tower height: 48 feet

Elevation of the focal
plane: 60 feet

Optic: Modern

Status: Active

Characteristic: Flashes
every 6 seconds

Range: 7 miles

Position: 47° 00' 12
90° 56' 12

Note: Volunteer keepers
offer tours during the
summer

TO SEE THE LIGHT: Although
less popular than Raspberry
and Michigan Islands, Sand
Island attracts its share of
summertime visitors. The
island can be reached via
water taxis, cruises, and
special tours available from
the Apostle Islands Cruise
Service; call (715)
779–3925 or (800)
323–7619. Visitors should
stop first at the lakeshore
headquarters, located in the
Old Courthouse in Bayfield,
Wisconsin. Write to Apostle
Islands National Lakeshore,
Chief of Interpretation, Route
1, P.O. Box 4, Bayfield, WI
54814; (715) 779–3398;
www.nps.gov/apis.

GITCHEE GUMEE: THE LAKE THAT SWALLOWED A THOUSAND SHIPS

Known to Midwestern Native American tribes as Gitchee Gumee, or "Great Water," and to the rest of us as Superior, it is one big lake. More than 350 miles long, 160 miles wide, and a quarter of a mile deep, it covers 31,200 square miles of the continental heartland in a cold, dark blanket of blue water. A liquid highway for freighters carrying ore, grain, chemicals, and cargo of every description, it is one of the most heavily traveled bodies of water on the planet. Even so, its shores include some of the most isolated places in America.

Ten percent of the earth's freshwater is locked up in this one huge lake. Another 10 percent can be found in the other four Great Lakes: Michigan, Huron, Erie, and Ontario. Together the five lakes impound approximately 5,500 cubic miles of water. To get an idea of what that means, consider the following. If the lakes were empty and the entire flow of the Mississippi could be diverted into them, it would take the Big Muddy more than fifty years to fill them up again. In reality these truly Great Lakes are inland seas.

Located near the center of the continent, the lakes are raked by giant weather systems and as a consequence are stormier than most of the world's oceans and seas. For hundreds of years sailors have battled the lakes' howling gales, and more than a few have perished in the fight. A single storm in 1913 shattered the hulls of more than forty ships and drowned at least 230 sailors. In all, the lakes have gobbled up at least 6,000 ships and drowned perhaps 50,000 passengers and crewmen. Many of these vessels disappeared without a trace. One such victim was the storm-blasted *Edmund Fitzgerald,* which took twenty-nine crewman to the bottom

of Lake Superior in 1975. As the *Fitzgerald* disaster illustrates, the losses have continued right down to our own times.

Fortunately, the dangers of navigating the lakes have not deterred seamen. Commerce on the Great Lakes has played an all-important role in the prosperous commercial development of the United States. We would be a much poorer nation without them. To understand why this is so, consider that a lake freighter of rather ordinary size can carry half a million bushels of wheat, enough for almost five million loaves of bread. It takes more than 20,000 acres of farm land to grow that much wheat in a year and at least twenty-five long railroad trains to haul it.

Longer, wider, and more northerly than its sisters, Superior is the stormiest and most dangerous of the lakes. Some would say it is also the most beautiful. Certainly its shores are more remote and pristine than those of the lower lakes. Like the other lakes, Superior is the child of glaciers that bulldozed great holes in the earth and when the climate turned warmer filled them with melt water. When you stand on the shore on any of the Apostle Islands and gaze out across Superior's nearly endless crystal waters, it is impossible to fully grasp the immensity of the treasure the glaciers left behind—nothing less than the greatest lake in the world.

Outer Island's 1875 fog-signal building is pictured here from the tower catwalk. As seen on the right, the tramway runs down to the dock, on the shore of Lake Superior.

One of the many attractions of Door County's Peninsula State Park, the Eagle Bluff Light Station houses a popular museum.
Rick Polad

Aids to Navigation Team

U.S. Coast Guard units assigned to operate and maintain light-houses, channel lights, buoys, and other maritime markers.

Automated light

A lighthouse with no keeper. Following World War II, remote control systems, light-activated switches, and fog-sensing devices made automation an increasingly cost-effective and attractive option, and the efficiency-minded U.S. Coast Guard automated one light station after another. By 1970, only about sixty U.S. lighthouses still had full-time keepers, and within two decades, all but one of those beacons had been automated. Appropriately enough, the historic Boston Harbor Lighthouse, automated in 1998, was the last to give up its keeper. All Wisconsin lights are automated.

Beacon

A light or radio signal intended to guide mariners or aviators.

Breakwater or pier light

Often harbors are protected from high waves by a lengthy barrier of stone called a breakwater. Because they rise only a few feet above the surface, breakwaters are hard to see, especially at night, and may threaten vessels entering or exiting the harbor. Breakwater beacons are meant to make mariners aware of this hazard so they may safely navigate the harbor entrance. For obvious reasons, the light tower usually is placed near the end of the breakwater.

Port Washington North Breakwater Light.

Cast-iron towers

Introduced as a building material during the 1840s, cast iron revolu-tionized lighthouse construction. Stronger than stone and relatively light, cast iron made it possible to fabricate the parts of a light tower in a far-off foundry and then ship them to the construction site for assembly. A cylindrical structure assembled in 1844 on Long Island Head in Boston Harbor may have been the first all cast-iron lighthouse.

Characteristic

The identifying feature of a lighthouse beacon. To help mariners tell one beacon from another, maritime officials gave each light a distinct color or pattern of flashes. For instance, the Sturgeon Bay Ship Canal Light flashes red every ten seconds, while the nearby pierhead light flashes red every two and one-half seconds, and the important Cana Island Light near the other end of the peninsula displays a fixed white light.

Clamshell or bivalve lenses

Most Fresnel lenses are round, but some have a slightly squeezed or flattened shape somewhat like that of a clamshell. They nearly always feature a pair of bull's-eyes or focal points, one on each side of the lens.

Clockwork mechanism

Early rotating lighthouse lenses were often driven by a set of gears, weights, and pulleys similar to those used in large clocks. Every few hours, the keeper had to "rewind" the machinery by pulling or cranking the weights to the top of the tower.

Coast Guard, United States

Since 1939, lighthouses and other aids to navigation in the United States have been the responsibility of the U.S. Coast Guard. Previously, the nation's maritime lights were maintained by a separate government agency known as the U.S. Lighthouse Service.

Elevation or height of the focal plane

Fresnel lenses and most modern optical systems channel light signals into a narrow band known as the focal plane. Because the curvature of the earth would render low-lying lights practically worthless for navigation, a coastal beacon must have an elevated focal plane. The height of the plane above the water's surface—usually from 40 to 200 feet—helps determine the range of the light.

Fixed signal

A lighthouse beacon that shines constantly during its regular hours of operation is said to display a fixed signal.

Flashing signal

A lighthouse beacon that turns on and off or grows much brighter at regular intervals is called a flashing signal.

Fog signal or foghorn

A distinct sound signal, usually a horn, trumpet, or siren, used to warn vessels away from prominent headlands or navigational obstacles during fog or other periods of low visibility.

Fresnel lenses

Invented in 1822 by Augustin-Jean Fresnel, a noted French physicist, Fresnel lenses concentrate light into a powerful beam that can be seen over great distances. Usually, they consist of individual hand-polished glass prisms arrayed in a bronze frame. Manufactured by a number of French and British companies, these devices came in as many as eleven different sizes or "orders." A massive first-order lens may be more than 6 feet in diameter and 12 feet tall, while a diminutive sixth-order lens is only about 1 foot wide and not much larger than an ordinary gallon jug.

Third-order Fresnel lens, Devils Island Light.

Gallery

A circular walkway with a railing around the lantern of a lighthouse. Galleries provided keepers convenient access to the outside of the lantern for window cleaning, painting, and repair work.

Harbor light

A beacon intended to assist vessels moving in and out of a harbor. Not meant to serve as major coastal markers, harbor lights often consisted of little more than a lantern hung from a pole. However, many were official light stations, with a tower and residence for the keeper.

Investigation of 1851

Following a rash of shipwrecks along the U.S. coast during the late 1840s and the collapse of the Minot's Ledge Lighthouse (Massachusetts) in 1851, Congress appointed a commission to investigate the nation's aids to navigation. Headed by Rear Admiral William B. Shubrick, the commission reported that the U.S. lighthouse system was at best shoddy and at worst a tragedy. In response, Congress handed authority over U.S. maritime aids to a nine-member Lighthouse Board headed by Shubrick himself.

Keeper

Before the era of automation, responsibility for operating and maintaining a light station was placed in the hands of a keeper, sometimes aided by one or more assistants. During the eighteenth and nineteenth centuries, keepers were appointed by the U.S. Treasury Department or even the president himself in return for military service or a political favor. Although the work was hard and the pay minimal, these appointments were coveted because they offered a steady income and free housing.

Keeper's residence or dwelling

The presence of a keeper's residence is what turned a light station into a light "house." Sometime keepers lived in the tower itself, but a typical lighthouse dwelling was a detached one-and-a-half-story wood or stone structure built in a style similar to that of other working-class homes in the area.

Lamp and reflector

For several decades prior to the introduction of the highly efficient Fresnel lens, lighthouse beacons were intensified by means of lamp-and-reflector systems. These combined a bright-burning lamp and a polished mirror shaped in a manner intended to concentrate the light.

Lantern

The glass-enclosed space at the top of a light tower is known as the lantern. It houses the lens or optic and protects it from the weather.

Light tower

A tall, often cylindrical structure used to elevate a navigational light so that mariners can see it from a distance. Modern light towers support a lantern, which houses a lamp, electric beacon, or some other lighting device. Some light towers are an integral part of the station residence, but most are detached.

Lighthouse

A term applied to a wide variety of buildings constructed for the purpose of guiding ships. Often it is used interchangeably with similar or derivative terms such as *light tower* or *light station*. Throughout this book you will often find the more general term *light* used in reference to individual lighthouses or light stations.

Lighthouse Board

Beginning in 1851 and for more than half a century afterwards, U.S. lighthouses were administered by a Lighthouse Board consisting of nine members. Usually board members were noted engineers, scientists, or military men. Creation of the board brought a fresh professional spirit and penchant for innovation to the Lighthouse Service. Perhaps the board's most telling change was adoption of the advanced Fresnel lens as the standard U.S. lighthouse optic.

Lighthouse Service

A common term applied to the various organizations or agencies that built and maintained U.S. lighthouses from 1789 until 1939, when the U.S. Coast Guard was placed in charge.

Lighthouse tenders

The U.S. Lighthouse Service and later the U.S. Coast Guard maintained a small fleet of freighters and work vessels to help build and supply lighthouses. They were vital to remote lighthouse stations and offshore towers, which otherwise would have been impossible to provision. By tradition, many lighthouse tenders were given the names of flowers, such as *Marigold* and *Amaranth*.

The tender "Amaranth" supplied light stations throughout the western Great Lakes during the early 1900s. U.S. Coast Guard

Lightships

Equipped with their own beacons, usually displayed from a tall central mast, lightships were essentially floating lighthouses. They marked shoals and key navigational turning points where construction of a permanent light tower was either impossible or prohibitively expensive.

Light station

A navigational facility with a light beacon is commonly referred to as a light station. Often the term is used interchangeably with *light-*

house, but a light station may or may not include a tower, quarters for a keeper, and a fog signal.

Modern optic

A term referring to a broad array of lightweight, mostly weatherproof devices that produce the most modern navigational lights.

Occulting or eclipsing light

There are several ways to produce a beacon that appears to flash. One is to "occult" or block the light at regular intervals, often with a rotating opaque panel.

Pleasonton, Stephen

A parsimonious Treasury Department auditor, Pleasonton took charge of the Lighthouse Service in 1820 and maintained a firm, if not stifling, grip on it for thirty years. Most historians agree that Pleasonton's tight-fistedness encouraged low construction standards and delayed U.S. adoption of advanced optical technology for many years.

Private aid to navigation

A privately owned and maintained navigational light. Often, such lights are formerly deactivated beacons that have been reestablished for historic or aesthetic purposes.

Range lights

Displayed in pairs, range lights help mariners keep their vessels safely within the narrow navigable channels that crisscross estuaries or lead in and out of harbors. The rear-range light is higher and farther from the water than its partner, the front-range light, which is often located at water's edge. When viewed from mid-channel, the lights appear in perfect vertical alignment. If the upper light tilts either to the right or the left, a helmsman must steer in the opposite direction to correct course.

Skeleton towers

Iron- or steel-skeleton light towers consist of four or more heavily braced metal legs topped by workrooms and/or a lantern. Relatively durable and inexpensive, they were built in considerable numbers during the latter half of the nineteenth century. Because their open walls offer little resistance to wind and water, these towers proved ideal for offshore navigational stations, but some, such as the soaring skeleton tower at Rawley Point near Two Rivers, Wisconsin, were built on land.

Solar-powered optic

Nowadays, many remote lighthouse beacons are powered by batteries recharged during the day by solar panels.

Wickies

Before electric power made lighthouse work much cleaner and simpler, nearly all navigational beacons were produced by oil or kerosene lamps. Most of these lamps had wicks that required constant care and trimming. Consequently, lighthouse keepers often referred to themselves somewhat humorously as "wickies."

ABOUT THE AUTHORS

Photographs by **Bruce Roberts** have appeared in numerous magazines, including *Life* and *Sports Illustrated*, and in hundreds of books, many of them about lighthouses. He was director of photography at *Southern Living* magazine for many years. His work is also on display in the permanent collection at the Smithsonian Institution. He lives in Morehead City, North Carolina.

Ray Jones is the author or coauthor of fourteen best-selling books about lighthouses. He has served as an editor at Time-Life Books, as founding editor of *Albuquerque Living* magazine, as writing coach at *Southern Living* magazine, and as founding publisher of Country Roads Press. He lives in Pebble Beach, California, where he continues to write about lighthouses and serves as a consultant to businesses, publishers, and other authors.

ALSO BY BRUCE ROBERTS AND RAY JONES

Lighthouses of California
A Guidebook and Keepsake

Lighthouses of Florida
A Guidebook and Keepsake

Lighthouses of Maine
A Guidebook and Keepsake

Lighthouses of Massachusetts
A Guidebook and Keepsake

Lighthouses of Michigan
A Guidebook and Keepsake

Lighthouses of New York
A Guidebook and Keepsake

Lighthouses of Washington
A Guidebook and Keepsake

New England Lighthouses
Maine to Long Island Sound

American Lighthouses
A Comprehensive Guide

Eastern Great Lakes Lighthouses
Ontario, Erie, and Huron

Western Great Lakes Lighthouses
Michigan and Superior

Gulf Coast Lighthouses
Florida Keys to the Rio Grande

Mid-Atlantic Lighthouses
Hudson River to Chesapeake Bay

Pacific Northwest Lighthouses
Oregon, Washington, Alaska, and British Columbia

Southern Lighthouses
Outer Banks to Cape Florida